impact
Foundation
Grammar Book

NATIONAL GEOGRAPHIC
L E A R N I N G

Australia · Brazil · Mexico · Singapore · United Kingdom · United States

impact
Foundation
Grammar Book

Be and *have got*

Countable and uncountable nouns

Explorers Max Lowe and Conrad Anker

Be and *have got*

We use the verb **be** for many things. We use it to talk about someone's nationality or name, or to give a description.
*My sister and I **are** interested in animals.*

In everyday English, we often use the shortened form.
*My brother**'s** crazy about animals, but I**'m not**.*

The question form reverses the order of the words.
***Is** your mum interested in animals?*

➔ See grammar box on page 52.

1 **Complete the sentences with the correct form of the verb *be*.**
You can use the short form.
Example: *I **am** very messy.* ✔

1. My brother _____ friendly. ✔
2. My grandfather _____ mean. ✗
3. My parents _____ very funny. ✗
4. My brother _____ sometimes annoying. ✔
5. My dad _____ good at cooking. ✔
6. My sister _____ good at maths. ✔
7. My grandmother _____ interested in football. ✗
8. My brothers _____ very noisy. ✔

2 (Circle) **the correct word.**
Example: (*I*) / *We am quite friendly.*

1. **They / He** are interested in animals.
2. Is **you / she** good at sport?
3. **We / He** are messy when we cook.
4. **He / I** is annoying.
5. **They / She** is funny.
6. **We / He** aren't crazy about crocodiles.
7. Is **he / you** noisy?
8. **We / He** isn't interested in football.

3 **Complete the questions with *Am, Are* or *Is*.** Then write the answers.
Example: ***Are*** *you interested in crocodiles?* ✔ ***Yes, I am.***

1. _____ there animals in a zoo? ✔   _____
2. _____ a crocodile a mammal? ✗   _____
3. _____ your brother interested in lions and tigers? ✔   _____
4. _____ I funny? ✔   _____
5. _____ your parents mean? ✗   _____
6. _____ your sister good at singing? ✔   _____
7. _____ your sisters noisy? ✔   _____
8. _____ we annoying when we ask questions? ✗   _____

We use **have got** to:

• show that something belongs to someone.

He's got crocodile posters.

• describe people, animals and things.

*Crocodiles **have got** sharp teeth.*

➔ See grammar box on page 52.

1 **Complete the sentences with the affirmative form of *have got*.**

Example: *I've got a pet dog.*

1. You _____ lots of toy lions and tigers.

2. They _____ a big garden.

3. My parents _____ two pet cats.

4. My brother _____ posters of crocodiles.

5. My dad _____ DVDs about giraffes.

6. My sister _____ two goldfish.

2 **Complete the sentences with the negative form of *have got*.**

Example: *I **haven't got** a pet lion!*

1. She _____ any children.

2. My parents _____ a pet dolphin.

3. My brother _____ many photographs of wild animals.

4. My cousin _____ any brothers or sisters.

5. They _____ any trees in their garden.

6. My mum _____ any books about crocodiles.

3 **Complete the questions with the correct form of *have got*.**

Example: ***Have you got** any pets? (you)*

1. _____ any brothers or sisters? (she)

2. _____ any books about animals? (your dad)

3. _____ a best friend? (your brother)

4. _____ a favourite food? (your mum)

5. _____ a boat? (your grandparents)

6. _____ anything on my hands? (I)

Countable and uncountable nouns

Nouns that we can count are called **countable nouns**. We can add an **-s** to make the noun plural. When the subject of a sentence is plural, the verb must also be plural.
*There **are ten candles** on the cake.*

We can put **a/an** or a number before a countable noun: **an** apple, **six** bottles.
Examples: *sandwich, biscuit, cake, grape, crisp*

Nouns that we cannot count and that do not have plurals are called **uncountable nouns**. We do not use **a/an** with uncountable nouns. When the subject of a sentence is an uncountable noun, the verb must be singular.
*The birthday party **food was** delicious.*
Examples: *bread, cheese, milk, tea, water*

We can use other words with uncountable nouns so that we know how much we have: *a slice of* (bread), *a piece of* (cheese), *a glass of* (milk), *a kilo of* (butter), *a plate of* (spaghetti).

We can use the word **some** in front of countable and uncountable nouns in affirmative sentences.
*There are **some** eggs in the box.*

We can use the word **any** in front of countable and uncountable nouns in negative sentences and questions.
*There aren't **any** dogs in the park.*
*Is there **any** milk left?*

---

1 **Complete the sentences with a, an or some.**

Example: *There are **some** candles on the cake.*

1. There's _____ cake on the table.

2. There's _____ water in the bottle.

3. There's _____ bottle of water on the table.

4. There are _____ cakes on the table.

5. I've got _____ grandfather.

6. My grandfather's got _____ old guitar.

7. Is there _____ apple in your bag?

8. Do your grandparents have _____ pet dog?

2 (Circle) the correct words.

Example: *Is /* (*Are*) *there any tomatoes in the fridge?*

1. The juice **is / are** freshly-squeezed.

2. The oranges **is / are** freshly-squeezed.

3. The strawberries **is / are** from the garden.

4. My brother's eyes **is / are** blue.

5. My cousin **isn't / aren't** interested in food.

6. There **is / are** a packet of crisps on the table.

7. There **isn't / aren't** any sugar in my coffee.

8. There **is / are** 30 children at this party.

3 (Circle) the correct words.

Example: *There is **a / an /*** (*some*) *milk in the fridge.*

1. Do you have **a / an / any** brothers or sisters?

2. Would you like **a / an / some** bread?

3. I would like **a / an / some** tea in the morning.

4. Would you like **a / an / some** plate of strawberries?

5. I have **a / an / some** grandmother in Mexico.

6. We live in **a / an / any** house in the north of England.

7. There's **a / an / some** fly in my soup!

8. There's **a / an / some** rice in the cupboard.

4 Complete the sentences with the words in the box.

an	any	apples	~~water~~	are	cheese	is	some	there

*Example: There is some **water** in the bottle.*

1. Are _____ enough biscuits?

2. _____ there any milk in the fridge?

3. Please can I have _____ orange?

4. There are _____ grapes on the table.

5. There _____ twelve bottles of water here.

6. We haven't got _____ coffee.

7. There are seven _____ on the tree.

8. There is some _____ on the plate.

Present simple

Adverbs of frequency

Children in a boat classroom, Bangladesh

Present simple: Talking about routines, habits and permanent states

We use the **present simple** to talk about:
- routines and habits.

*I **eat** lunch at school during the week.*

*My father **goes** to the supermarket every Saturday.*

- permanent states.

*My brother **is** tall.*

➔ See grammar box on page 52.

1 **Write the third person singular of the verbs.**

Example: *get up*   ***gets up***

1. go _____

2. drink _____

3. finish _____

4. do _____

5. open _____

6. eat _____

7. make _____

8. hang out _____

2 **Circle the correct form of the verb.**

Example: *I (eat) / eats breakfast with my family.*

1. My sister **get up / gets up** at seven o'clock on weekdays.

2. My mother **drink / drinks** tea at breakfast.

3. We **go / goes** to school by bus.

4. I **go / goes** home for lunch.

5. My brother and sister **don't / doesn't** eat at home.

6. My father **make / makes** my lunch.

7. I **return / returns** to school after lunch.

8. Classes **finish / finishes** at 3.30 p.m.

3 **Tick the correct sentences.** Rewrite the incorrect sentences.

Example: *Does you eat breakfast every day?* ✗
         ***Do** you eat breakfast every day?*

1. I plays in the park after school.   _____ _____

2. My grandad is very old.   _____ _____

3. Every year, we goes to Spain on holiday.   _____ _____

4. I get up at seven o'clock.   _____ _____

5. There are a good library near my house.   _____ _____

6. Do you likes pizza?   _____ _____

4 **Complete the text with the correct form of the verb in brackets.**

My name _____is_____ (be) Ana and I am 11 years old. I [1]_____ (live) in Rosario in

Argentina with my brothers Eduardo and Guillermo, and my parents. We [2]_____ (get up) every

morning at half past six and my father [3]_____ (prepare) breakfast for the family. After breakfast,

my mother [4]_____ (go) to work and we [5]_____ (leave) for school on the bus.

My father [6]_____ (take) us to the bus stop. He then [7]_____ (walk) to his office.

At lunch, we [8]_____ (eat) at school. School [9]_____ (finish) at 4 p.m. My brother

Eduardo and I [10]_____ (do) sport after school twice a week.

We [11]_____ (return) home after school and do our homework. My brother Guillermo sometimes

[12]_____ (do) his homework at school.

5 **Complete the sentences with the correct form of the verb in brackets.**

Example: *They **eat** breakfast later on Saturdays. (eat)*

1. My brothers and I _____ late on Sundays. (get up)

2. My mother and father _____ coffee at weekends. (drink)

3. My father and I _____ to the supermarket on Saturdays. (go)

4. I _____ fast food for lunch on Saturdays. (eat)

5. My brother _____ burgers. (like)

6. My mother and father _____ dinner together. (make)

7. I _____ my homework on Sunday evenings. (finish)

8. My father and brother Eduard _____ lots of sport on television. (watch)

Adverbs of frequency: Saying how often you do something

We use **adverbs of frequency** to talk about habits or when we want to say how often something happens. The one-word adverbs of frequency are:

0% ⟵————————————————————⟶ 100%

never   **rarely**   **sometimes**   **often**   **always**

Adverbs of frequency come before the main verb, unless the verb is *be*.
*I **often** go online.*
*He **always** eats a sandwich for lunch.*
*I am **always** late for school.*

We can use time expressions such as *every day, every month, once a week* and *on Mondays* to say how often we do something. They usually go at the beginning or the end of a sentence.
*He walks to work **every day**.*
***On Mondays**, she plays basketball.*

1 (Circle) the correct adverb of frequency.

Example: *I eat cereal for breakfast every day.* (**sometimes** / (**always**))

1. I go to the gym twice a year. (**rarely** / **often**)

2. I don't go to the cinema unless there is a really good film on. (**never** / **sometimes**)

3. I play football three times a week. (**often** / **sometimes**)

4. My family eat together every Sunday. (**sometimes** / **always**)

5. My grandmother checks her emails once a month. (**rarely** / **often**)

6. I get up at seven o'clock five days a week. (**often** / **always**)

2 Put the words in the correct order.

Example: *my grandfather / online / goes / never*   ***My grandfather never goes online.***

1. late / my friends / for school / never / are   _____

2. my teacher / wears / often / jacket / the same   _____

3. takes me / my dad / rarely / to school   _____

4. play / you / on Saturdays / do / always / football?   _____

5. rarely / I / for lunch / go out   _____

6. finish / always / lunch / my / I   _____

3 **Look at the table.** Make sentences with the adverbs of frequency.

	go online	play tennis	go for a walk
Me	every day	often	rarely
My brother	often	sometimes	never
My mother	four times a month	every Tuesday	often
My father	sometimes	never	sometimes

Example: *I go online every day.* (I / go online)

1. _____ (I / tennis)

2. _____ (My mother / play tennis)

3. _____ (My brother / go for a walk)

4. _____ (My father / play tennis)

5. _____ (I / go for a walk)

6. _____ (My brother / go online)

7. _____ (My father / go for a walk)

8. _____ (My mother / go online)

4 **Complete the dialogue with the words in the box.**

often   always   every   sometimes   never

A: How ____*often*____ do you go to the cinema?

B: I go ¹ _____ Monday. I ² _____ go at the weekend, too. How often do you go to the cinema?

A: I ³ _____ go at the weekend. I ⁴ _____ go in the week, as I am too busy with homework.

WRITING

Write sentences about yourself.

1. I always _____ .

2. I often _____ .

3. I sometimes _____ .

4. I rarely _____ .

5. I never _____ .

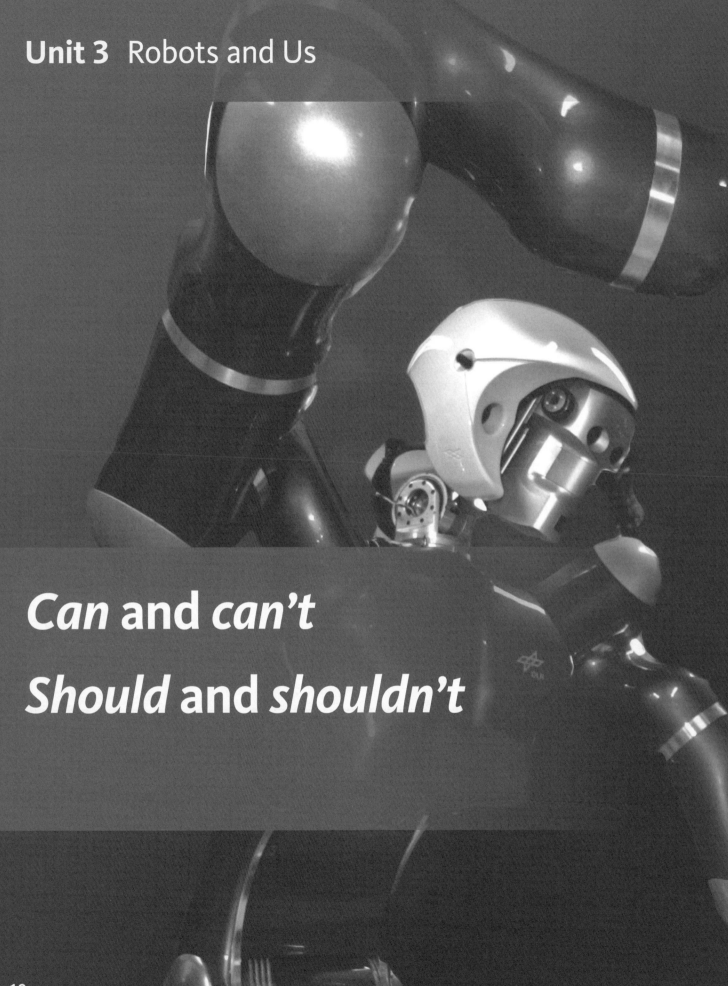

Can and *can't*
Should and *shouldn't*

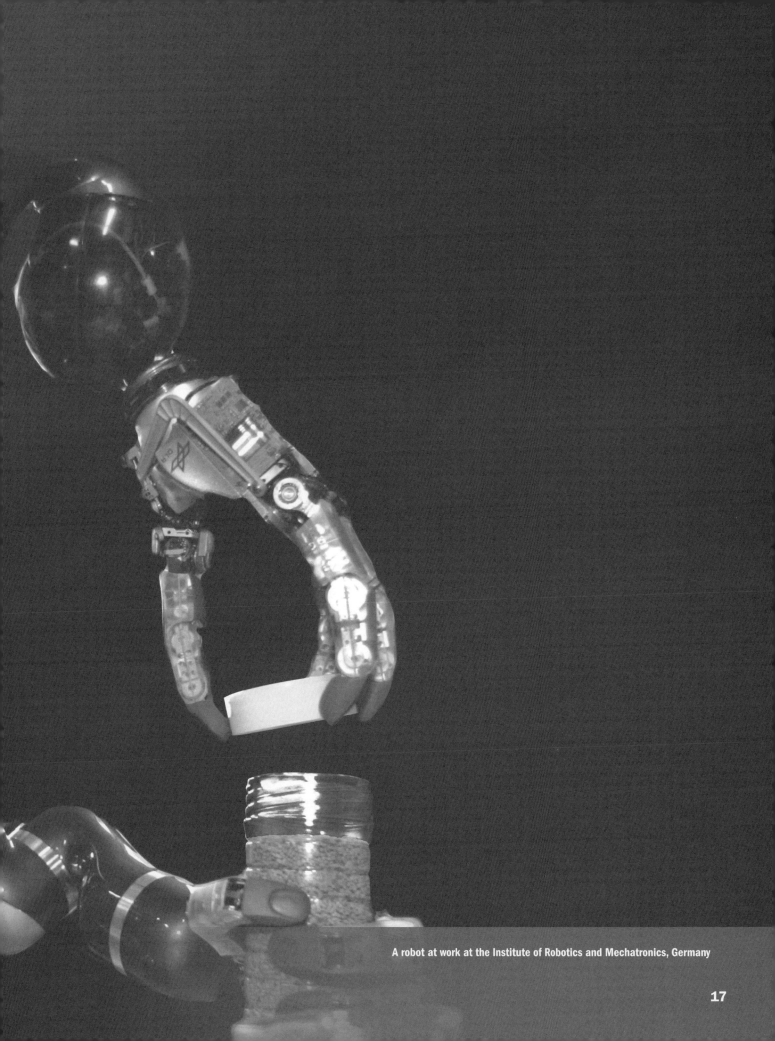

A robot at work at the Institute of Robotics and Mechatronics, Germany

Can and *can't:* Talking about ability

We use **can** and **can't** to talk about ability. They are followed by a bare infinitive.

*I **can't** sing.*

*You **can** speak English.*

***Can** he swim?*

*Yes, he **can**./No, he **can't**.*

We also use **can** to ask for or give permission to do something.

***Can** I borrow your pen?*

*You **can't** use your books in a test.*

1 **Complete the sentences with *can* or *can't* and the verb in brackets.**

Example: *My robot **can speak** French. (speak)*

1. _____ you _____ Chinese? (speak)

2. Robots _____ books. (not read)

3. Robots _____ instructions. (follow)

4. My robotic pet dog _____ . (bark)

5. _____ your house cleaning robot _____ clothes? (wash)

6. _____ your robot _____ ? (sing)

7. My sister's robot _____ her voice. (recognise)

8. My brother's robotic pet fish _____ very well! (not swim)

2 **Match the questions to the answers.**

1. Can you speak French?
2. Can you run fast?
3. Can you play the piano?
4. Can you play a musical instrument?
5. Can you play tennis?
6. Can you use a smartphone?
7. Can you ride a horse?
8. Can you sing well?
9. Can you cook?
10. Can your brother code?

a. No, but I can play the violin.
b. Yes, but I prefer using my tablet.
c. Yes, I can. But not very well.
d. Yes. I can ride a bike, too.
e. No, but I can play squash.
f. No, but my brother can. He plays the guitar.
g. No, but my sister can.
h. Yes, I make good cakes.
i. I can sing, but not very well.
j. No, but I can swim fast.

3 **Put the dialogue in the correct order.**

_____ 'I can play football, tennis and golf. I can't swim very well.'

_____ 'Yes, I can, but not very fast. I prefer surfing. What sports can you play?'

_____ 'I can speak English, Spanish and Chinese. Can you swim?'

___1___ 'Which languages can you speak?'

_____ 'I can speak English, French and Arabic. What about you?'

4 **Use the prompts to write questions and answers.**

Example: *you / swim?* ✔

       Can you swim? Yes, I can.

1. your brother / cook? ✔

_____   _____

2. you / play the piano? ✗

_____   _____

3. your robot / understand me? ✔

_____   _____

4. we / go to the cinema? ✔

_____   _____

5. I / borrow your car, Dad? ✗

_____   _____

6. you / dance? ✗

_____   _____

7. your mum / sing? ✔

_____   _____

8. I / wash the dishes? ✔

_____   _____

WRITING

Write sentences about yourself.

Example: *I **can** speak French, but I **can't** speak German.*

1. I can speak _____, but I can't speak _____ .

2. I can play _____, but I can't play _____ .

3. I can eat _____, but I can't eat _____ .

4. I can ride _____, but I can't ride _____ .

Should and *shouldn't*: Giving advice

We use *should* and *shouldn't*:
- to give advice.

I/You/He/She/It/We/You/They **should/shouldn't** watch television.
- to ask for advice.

Should *I do my homework tonight? Yes, you* **should.**/*No, you* **shouldn't.**

REMEMBER

There is no *s* in the third person: *should* NOT *shoulds*.

Should is a modal verb and is followed by a bare infinitive — there is no *to* before the verb.

You should read this book. NOT *You should ~~to~~ read this book.*

1 Complete the sentences using *should* or *shouldn't* with the correct verb from the box.

| ~~choose~~ | train | eat | sleep | remain | find | practise | have | try |

Example: *You* **should choose** *a sport you love.*

Do you want to be a professional athlete?

You:

1. _____ junk food.

2. _____ at least eight hours a night.

3. _____ a good coach.

4. _____ the things you find most difficult in the sport, not the easiest.

5. _____ a rest day every week.

6. _____ on your own – it's better to have a team or a partner.

7. _____ positive when you get injured.

8. _____ to take short cuts – that is often how you get injured.

2 **Find the mistakes in each sentence.** Rewrite the sentences.

Example: *I think you should to learn how to code.*
I think you should learn how to code.

1. They should to read more books.

   _____

2. He shoulds ask for my advice.

   _____

3. Do we should go to the cinema?

   _____

4. You don't should pay so much to download music.

   _____

5. We should to join a computer club.

   _____

6. What shoulds she study at university?

   _____

7. Do we should to study maths?

   _____

3 (Circle) the correct option.

Example: Example: A: *I really like that song.*
B: *You* (**should**)/ **shouldn't** *download it.*

1. A: This skirt is dirty.
   B: You **should / shouldn't** wear it to school.

2. A: I am really thirsty!
   B: You **should / shouldn't** drink a glass of water.

3. A: I have had such a big lunch!
   B: You **should / shouldn't** eat any dessert then.

4. A: I am interested in technology.
   B: You **should / shouldn't** go to the new science museum.

5. A: I love your dress.
   B: You **should / shouldn't** borrow it for the party.

6. A: I don't know if I like broccoli.
   B: You **should / shouldn't** try it.

7. A: I enjoy all sports.
   B: You **should / shouldn't** come to my tennis class.

WRITING

Write some advice for yourself.

Example: *I **can't** play tennis very well, so I **should** practise more.*

Quantifiers
Adverbs

Butterflies on the shoreline of the Juruena River, Brazil

Quantifiers: Talking and asking about quantity

We use **much** and **(a) little** with uncountable nouns.
*A camel doesn't drink **much** water.*
*There is very **little** water in the desert.*

We use **many**, **(a) few**, **a lot (of)** and **lots (of)** with countable nouns.
*There aren't **many** trees in the desert.*
*There are **few** plants in the desert.*
*There are **lots of** camels here.*
*We have bought **a lot of** camels.*

When we ask questions about quantity, we use **how much** for uncountable nouns and **how many**
for countable nouns.
***How much** money do we have?*
***How many** camels can we buy?*

1 **Complete the questions with *much* or *many*.**

Example: *How **much** do camels eat?*

1. How _____ humps has a Bactrian camel got?

2. How _____ wild Bactrian camels are there in the world?

3. How _____ water can a camel drink?

4. How _____ animal species live in the desert?

5. How _____ time does a camel spend looking for food every day?

6. How _____ camels do you own?

2 **Circle the correct answer.**

Example: *There is **much** / a lot of sand in the desert.*

1. There is **little** / **few** water in the desert.

2. There are **many** / **much** conservation projects which help endangered animals.

3. Some plants keep **many** / **a lot of** water in their leaves.

4. Lions have **few** / **little** predators.

5. Pandas eat **a lot of** / **few** bamboo every day.

6. How **much** / **many** times have you worn a panda costume?

7. They didn't spend **much** / **many** time in the desert.

8. Only **a little** / **a few** people are allowed to work with pandas.

3 (Circle) the correct answer.

Example: _____ of animals are born in captivity.　　a. *Few*　(b.) *A lot*　c. *Little*

1. There are _____ of trees in the rain forest.　　a. few　b. a little　c. a lot

2. There are _____ poisonous spiders in Europe.　　a. few　b. lots　c. little

3. Do camels drink _____ of water?　　a. a few　b. a lot　c. a little

4. There's _____ time left to save the rhinos.　　a. few　b. little　c. a lot

5. Cacti are plants that need _____ water.　　a. little　b. few　c. lots

6. _____ different species of leopard live in those mountains.　　a. A little　b. A lot　c. A few

4 **Read.** Complete the text with *much*, *many*, *a lot*, *little* or *few*.

There is very ____little____ water in a desert, but there is ¹_____ of water in a rain

forest. ²_____ animals find it easy to live in a desert because of the difficult conditions.

However, there are ³_____ different species of animals in a rain forest.

There aren't ⁴_____ trees in a desert, so there isn't ⁵_____ shade.

However, there are ⁶_____ of trees in a rain forest which provide ⁷_____ of

shade. For this reason, ⁸_____ different animals make their homes in a rain forest.

5 **Are these quantifiers correct?** Tick the correct sentences. Rewrite the incorrect sentences.

Example: *How much pandas live in the sanctuary?* ✘

*　　**How many** pandas live in the sanctuary?*

1. There aren't few rhinos left in the wild. _____

_____

2. They spent a lot of money trying to protect the birds. _____

_____

3. There wasn't many snow in the mountains. _____

_____

4. The guide gave us little advice. _____

_____

5. There were a lot of signs in the zoo. _____

_____

6. Hurry up! We haven't got little time. _____

_____

Adverbs: Saying how you do something

Adverbs describe how we do something.
She drives her car **carefully**.

We usually make adverbs by adding *-ly* to the adjective.
quick ⟶ *quickly*

When the adjective ends in *-y*, we take off the *-y* and add *-ily*.
easy ⟶ *easily*

When the adjective ends in *-le*, we take off the *-e* and add *-y*.
simple ⟶ *simply*

Some adverbs don't end in *-ly* and have the same form as the adjective.

hard	⟶ *hard*		*early*	⟶ *early*
fast	⟶ *fast*		*late*	⟶ *late*

Some adverbs don't end in *-ly* and have a different form from the adjective.
good ⟶ *well*

Adverbs that describe how we do something usually go after the main verb.
He runs **quickly** *around the park every morning.*

REMEMBER

Adjectives describe what a noun does and adverbs describe a verb.

adjective	adverb	adjective	adverb	adjective	adverb	adjective	adverb
good ⟶	well	high ⟶	high	easy ⟶	easily	hard ⟶	hard
fast ⟶	fast	bad ⟶	badly	gentle ⟶	gently	loud ⟶	loudly

1 **Read.** Make sentences using an adverb and the verb in brackets.

Example: *Monkeys are good climbers. (climb)*
Monkeys **climb** *very* **well**.

1. My tortoise is slow. (walk) _____

2. The train is fast. (go) _____

3. I am good at rugby. (play) _____

4. My sister is good at the guitar. (play) _____

5. My brother is loud. (shout) _____

6. My dad has a gentle voice. (speak) _____

2 **Make sentences about the people below and their abilities.** Use *can* and *can't* from Unit 3.

Example: ***A cyclist can cycle very fast.***

swimmer   violinist   footballer

television presenter   scientist

climber   artist   marathon runner

baby   cyclist

well	skilfully	clearly
carefully	beautifully	high
fast	easily	loudly

1. _____
2. _____
3. _____
4. _____
5. _____
6. _____
7. _____
8. _____
9. _____
10. _____

3 **Complete the text with words from the box.** Use each word once.

~~many~~   actively   few   a lot of   much   a lot   little   quickly

There are ___many___ different animals that live in the desert. There is not [1]_____ water or grass in the desert, so how do these animals survive? Some animals eat cacti, which hold [2]_____ of water. Other animals, such as kangaroo rats, sleep in the daytime and [3]_____ hunt for food at night. They spend very [4]_____ time above ground. They prefer to stay in underground tunnels where the temperatures are lower. This is because their bodies heat up [5]_____ and it is dangerous for mammals to get too hot. [6]_____ animals also drink as much water as possible when they find it. [7]_____ animals do this better than the camel.

Present continuous

There was and *there were*

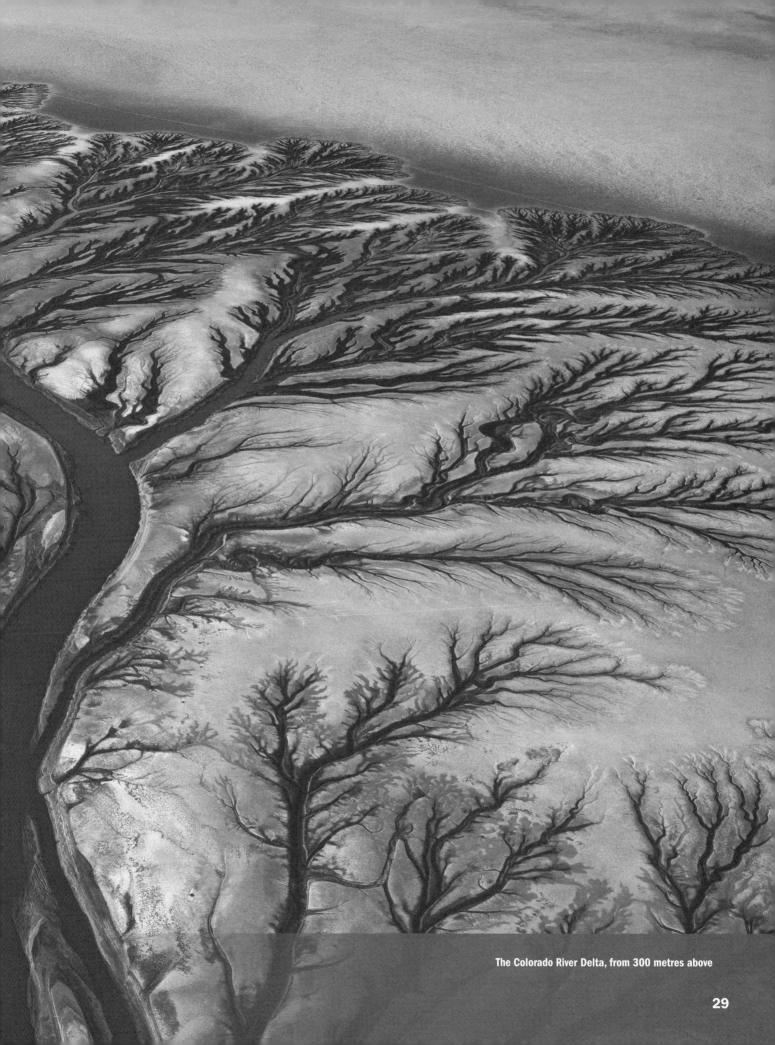

The Colorado River Delta, from 300 metres above

Present continuous: Talking about what is happening now and things that always happen

We use the **present continuous** to talk about:
- things that are in progress at the time of speaking.

*What **are** they **doing**? They**'re talking** to each other.*
- things that are in progress around the time of speaking or that are temporary.

*He**'s buying** a new car.*
- changing situations.

*My English **is improving**.*
- things that always happen.

*My sister is **always** buying clothes!*

The present continuous is formed with *be* + verb + *-ing*.
When the main verb ends in *-e*, we take off the *-e* and add *-ing*.

make ⟶ *making*

When the verb ends in a consonant and before that consonant there is a vowel, we double the final consonant and add *-ing*.

put ⟶ *putting*

When the verb ends in *-l*, we double the *-l* and add *-ing*.

cancel ⟶ *cancelling*

When the verb ends in *-ie*, we take off the *-ie* and add *-y* and *-ing*.

tie ⟶ *tying*
lie ⟶ *lying*

We can use time expressions such as *now, at the moment, these days, at present, today,* etc. with the present continuous. *She**'s doing** her homework **at the moment**.*

➔ See grammar box on page 53.

---

1 **Make the *-ing* form of the verb.** Then write the words in the correct column.

~~buy~~	get	have	talk	propel	plant	make	shake	die
	run	speak	walk	travel	win	sit	lie	bake

help ⟶ helping	put ⟶ putting	take ⟶ taking	tie ⟶ tying	cancel ⟶ cancelling
buying				

2 **Complete the sentences with the affirmative form of the present continuous.** Use the verb in brackets.

Example: *I **am helping** my sister. (help)*

1. We _____ how to save water. (learn)

2. I _____ trees and flowers in the garden. (plant)

3. My mum _____ us not to watch so much TV. (always tell)

4. My brother _____ less often. (shower)

5. I _____ not to waste water. (try)

3 **Complete the sentences with the negative form of the present continuous.** Use the verb in brackets.

Example: *My little brother **isn't helping** us much. (help)*

1. He _____ off the kitchen tap. (turn)

2. He _____ . (listen)

3. It _____ us, as he is too young to understand. (annoy)

4. So we _____ him off. (tell)

5. We _____ as much water as before. (waste)

6. My parents _____ bottled water any more. (buy)

7. My brother and I _____ pocket money for washing dad's car. (get)

4 **Use the prompts to write sentences in the present continuous.**

Example: *my dad / not water / the plants as much*
   My dad is not watering the plants as much.

1. my sister / not take / as much time in the shower

   _____

2. our dad / always complain / about how much water we use

   _____

3. my parents / put / bricks in the water tanks

   _____

4. we / use / water from the roof

   _____

5. we / not buy / bottled water

   _____

6. my friends / try / to save water, too

   _____

There was and *there were*: Talking about the past

We use ***there was*** and ***there were*** to talk or ask about what existed in the past.
There was *pollution in the water.*
There were *a lot of dead fish in the river.*

➔ See grammar box on page 53.

1 (Circle) the correct word.

Example: *When my dad was younger, there* (**wasn't**) / **weren't** *a tap in the village.*

1. I fell over because there **was** / **were** ice on the pavement.

2. There **wasn't** / **weren't** any clouds in the sky yesterday.

3. There **wasn't** / **weren't** any rainwater in the container.

4. The pilot couldn't take off because there **was** / **were** too much fog.

5. There **was** / **were** lots of interest in the campaign.

6. There **was** / **were** a lot of sunshine last week.

7. There **wasn't** / **weren't** much rainfall during the summer.

8. There **wasn't** / **weren't** any details about the disaster.

9. There **was** / **were** an oil spill in the ocean last year.

10. There **was** / **were** plenty of people on the beaches, trying to save the birds.

2 Complete the sentences with *There was/wasn't* or *There were/weren't*.

Example: ***There were*** *a lot of plastic bottles for sale in the shops.* ✔

1. _____ a water supply in the village. ✘

2. _____ any fish in the rivers. ✘

3. _____ as much pollution as there is today. ✘

4. _____ terrible floods in the 1950s. ✔

5. _____ a lot of plastic beads in the sea. ✔

6. _____ anything we could do to help. ✘

7. _____ a campaign at school to reduce waste. ✔

8. _____ too many people without clean water. ✔

9. _____ a drought during the 1980s. ✔

10. _____ any turtles on the beach last night. ✘

3 **Read.** Tick *T* for *true* or *F* for *false*. Correct the false sentences.

Even today, there are lots of remote towns and villages which haven't got any fresh water. I live in a remote village in India. In the 1950s, when my parents were young, there wasn't a clean water supply in our village. There was one tap in a village six kilometres away. My mum remembers walking there to collect clean water for her family. It was a daily chore. She didn't enjoy it because there were snakes on the path and she was scared of them. She also told me that many villagers fell ill from the dirty water. However, in 1994, a fresh water pipe was installed into the village. Now, every villager has got a tap in their home and people don't often get ill.

1. Nowadays, there is fresh water in all villages and towns.   (T) (F)

_____

2. There wasn't clean water in the writer's village in the 1950s.   (T) (F)

_____

3. There was one tap in the writer's village in the 1950s.   (T) (F)

_____

4. There weren't any dangers on the path to fetch fresh water.   (T) (F)

_____

5. There was a lot of illness before the villages had clean water.   (T) (F)

_____

6. Before 1994, there weren't taps in people's homes.   (T) (F)

_____

WRITING

Write sentences to describe:

1. a past problem. Use *there was*, *there were*, *there wasn't* or *there weren't*.
2. a solution to the problem. Use the present continuous.

Past simple

Moscow, Russia, at night

Past simple: Talking about the past

We use the **past simple** to talk about:
- things in the past which have finished.

*I **went** on holiday last year.*
- things in the past which were habits.

*Last year, I **swam** every morning before breakfast.*
- things in the past which happened one after the other.

*She **got** in the car, **turned** the key and **drove** away.*

We form the past simple affirmative of regular verbs by adding the -ed ending.

work ⟶ worked

When the verb ends in -e, we add -d.

bake ⟶ baked

When the verb ends in a consonant and -y, we take off the -y and add -ied.

carry ⟶ carried

➔ See grammar box on page 53.

There are many irregular verbs in English. We do not form the past simple of these verbs by adding -ed.

➔ See the irregular verbs list on page 54.

1 **Read the school trip diary entries.** Look at sentences 1–8. Tick *T* for *True* or *F* for *False*.

20th January	Arrive in Armenia
21st January	Rest day and visits to local sites
22nd January	Visit the monastery to set up 3D scanning equipment
23rd January	Begin scanning the first part of the site
24th January	Move the equipment to new wing of monastery
25th January	Finish scanning and pack up equipment
26th January	Pack up / go home

1. We visited the monastery on the day we arrived in Armenia.   (T) (F)

2. We visited local monuments on the second day.   (T) (F)

3. We began scanning the site on the third day.   (T) (F)

4. We first arrived at the monastery on the third day.   (T) (F)

5. On the fourth day, we moved to a different monastery.   (T) (F)

6. On the fifth day, we were in another part of the monastery.   (T) (F)

7. On the sixth day, we ate a meal in the evening.   (T) (F)

8. On the seventh day, we went home.   (T) (F)

2 **Which of these are correct?** Rewrite the incorrect words.

Example: *tryed* ✗ *tried*

1. played _____
2. lifted _____
3. visitted _____
4. traveled _____

5. qualifyed _____
6. learnt _____
7. carried _____
8. scanned _____

3 **Read.** Complete the text with the past simple form of the verb in brackets.

2001	Finish school
2001	Start university
2005	Graduate with French degree
2005–2006	Travel around West Africa
2006–2007	Study for teaching certificate
2007	Start teaching French

I ___finished___ (finish) school in 2001 and I ¹_____ (start) university later that year.

After I ²_____ (graduate) from university with a degree in French, I ³_____ (go)

overseas. I ⁴_____ (travel) around West Africa for seven months. After that I ⁵_____

(study) for a qualification in teaching. In 2007, I ⁶_____ (begin) teaching in a language school.

4 **Put the words in the correct order.**

Example: *went / yesterday / cinema / the / I / to*
   I went to the cinema yesterday.

1. Spain / family / visited / I / year / last / with

_____

2. we / to / in the / London / went / summer

_____

3. ate / in / meal / restaurant / a / a / nice / we

_____

4. learnt / my / some / friend / on / Spanish / holiday

_____

5. us / my / the / took / to / parents / beach

_____

6. they / at / rented / beach / the / surfboards

_____

Past simple: Asking questions about the past

We use **did** for questions in the past simple, when we want to find out information.
*Where **did** you go last summer?*
We went to Beijing.
*What **did** you do?*
We visited the National Centre for the Performing Arts.

We use **didn't** for negative questions in the past simple, when we want confirmation.
***Didn't** you go by plane?*
*No, we **didn't**. We went by train.*

➔ See grammar box on page 53.

1 **Complete the questions with the past simple.**

Example: ***Did you enjoy*** *your trip to Spain? (you / enjoy)*

1. _____ to Madrid? (you / fly)

2. _____ the food there? (your parents / like)

3. _____ any museums? (you / visit)

4. _____ to a bull fight? (you / go)

5. _____ a tour of the Real Madrid stadium? (your brother / do)

6. _____ late? (the locals / eat)

7. _____ a favourite moment? (you / have)

8. _____ to come home? (you / want)

2 **Write answers to the questions in Activity 1.**

Example: ***Yes, we did.***

1. ✔ _____

2. ✔ _____

3. ✔ _____

4. ✗ _____

5. ✔ _____

6. ✔ _____

7. ✔ _____

8. ✗ _____

3 **Use the prompts to write questions in the past simple.**

Example: *you / go to Italy / last year*
Did you go to Italy last year?

1. he / buy a present / for his mother / in Spain

_____

2. you / enjoy / spending time / with your family

_____

3. you / walk around / the city

_____

4. they / fly back to London / last night

_____

5. she / arrive / yesterday

_____

6. it / rain in Spain / last week

_____

7. you / watch a football match / in Madrid

_____

8. you / speak any Italian / in Italy

_____

4 **Write answers to the questions in Activity 3.**

Example: **No, I didn't.**

1. ✗ _____
2. ✔ _____
3. ✔ _____
4. ✗ _____
5. ✗ _____
6. ✗ _____
7. ✗ _____
8. ✔ _____

WRITING

Write the text of an interview with a friend or family member about their last holiday.

Example: *Q: Did you go to France last year?*

A: Yes, we did. We went during the summer holidays.

Comparatives
Superlatives

NASA astronaut Mike Hopkins on a spacewalk

Comparatives: Comparing two things

We use the **comparative form** to compare two people, animals or things. We often use the word **than** after the comparative form.

She's **taller than** me.

This museum is **more interesting than** the other one.

To make the comparative form of adjectives with one syllable, we add the ending -er.

small ⟶ smaller

When the adjective ends in -e, we just add -r.

close ⟶ closer

When the adjective ends in a vowel and a consonant, we double the last consonant and add -er.

big ⟶ bigger

When the adjective ends in -y, we take off the -y and add -ier.

early ⟶ earlier

We use the word more with two-syllable (and longer) adjectives to make the comparative form.

interesting ⟶ more interesting

Some two-syllable adjectives have two comparative forms.

simple ⟶ simpler/more simple

clever ⟶ cleverer/more clever

polite ⟶ politer/more polite

We use the word more to make the comparative form of adjectives with three or more syllables.

confusing ⟶ more confusing

Some adjectives are irregular and do not follow these rules.

good ⟶ better

bad ⟶ worse

1 **Complete the sentences with the comparative form of the adjective in brackets.**

Example: Saturn is **bigger than** Earth. (big)

1. A ship is _____ a plane. (slow)

2. Her children are _____ mine. (old)

3. She's _____ her daughter. (small)

4. The football fans were _____ I expected. (loud)

5. Spain is _____ England. (warm)

6. My dog is _____ yours. (big)

7. A motorbike is _____ a bicycle. (fast)

8. This kitten is _____ that cat. (young)

2 **Complete the sentences with an adjective from the box in the comparative.**

| bad | big | clear | comfortable | ~~early~~ | good | hot | important | quiet |

Example: *Sam arrived at the museum* **earlier than** *Kate.*

1. Dad's food is _____ Mum's. Mum's is delicious.

2. I think trainers are _____ boots.

3. The new engine is _____ the old one. You can hardly hear it at all.

4. My grandma says that being kind is _____ being successful.

5. Suzie is _____ me at science.

6. Some squid are _____ cars!

7. Why is Venus _____ Mercury when Mercury is closer to the sun?

8. My instructions are much _____ yours. Yours are very difficult to read.

3 **Answer the following questions in the negative, using a different comparative adjective.**

Example: *Is a car faster than a motorbike?*
        No, a car is slower than a motorbike.

1. Is an elephant taller than a giraffe?

   _____

2. Is Earth further from the sun than Saturn?

   _____

3. Is a leopard heavier than a lion?

   _____

4. Is a gazelle faster than a cheetah?

   _____

5. Is England warmer than Spain?

   _____

6. Are donkeys bigger than horses?

   _____

7. Are you older than your sister?

   _____

8. Is geography more interesting than history?

   _____

WRITING

Make comparisons between you and a friend. For each comparison, write two statements.

Example: *Sarah is* **older than** *me. I am* **younger than** *Sarah.*

Superlatives: Comparing three or more things

We use the **superlative form** to compare three or more people, animals or things. We often use a phrase beginning with *in* or *of* to continue the sentence.
*She's **the tallest** in her class.*

To make the superlative form of adjectives with one syllable, we add the ending *-est*. We use the word *the* before the adjective in its superlative form.

tall   ⟶   *the tallest*

When the adjective ends in *-e*, we just add *-st*.

late   ⟶   *the latest*

When the adjective ends in a vowel and a consonant, we double the last consonant and add *-est*.

fit   ⟶   *the fittest*

When the adjective ends in *-y*, we take off the *-y* and add *-iest*.

happy   ⟶   *the happiest*

We usually use *the most* with a two-syllable adjective to make the superlative form.

famous ⟶   *the most famous*

Some two-syllable adjectives have two superlative forms.

simple   ⟶   *the simplest/the most simple*
clever   ⟶   *the cleverest/the most clever*
polite   ⟶   *the politest/the most polite*

We use the word *most* to make the superlative form of adjectives with three or more syllables.

confusing ⟶   *the most confusing*

Some adjectives are irregular and do not follow these rules.

good   ⟶   *the best*
bad   ⟶   *the worst*

1 **The words in bold are incorrect.** Write them correctly.

Example: *Tomas is the **goodest** swimmer in the class.*   ***best***

1. Dad is the **talest** in our family.   _____

2. My friend Lina is the **happyest** person I know.   _____

3. This is **a** simplest maths test.   _____

4. That restaurant is the **worse** in town.   _____

5. This is the **mostest** delicious cake.   _____

6. Who is the **oldst** person you know?   _____

2 **Complete the sentences with the superlative form of the adjective in brackets.**

Example: *My friend Ana is **the cleverest** person in my class. (clever)*

1. She knows _____ facts about space. (interesting)

2. Her project was _____ one in the class. (good)

3. She wrote about _____ stars to Earth. (close)

4. It was _____ subject, but she made it easy to understand. (difficult)

5. She's _____ of four sisters. (old)

6. My project was voted _____ in the class. (original)

3 **Change the adjectives into superlatives.** Then make sentences with them.

Example: *silly* ———→ ***silliest*** ———→ ***It was the silliest idea.***

1. good   _____

2. bad   _____

3. funny _____

4. sad   _____

5. happy _____

6. big   _____

7. interesting _____

4 **Complete the sentences with a superlative and *the* or *my*.**

Example: *It's a very big planet. It's **the biggest** in the solar system.*

1. Pluto is very far away. It's _____ planet from our sun.

2. I am good at science. It's _____ subject.

3. Mr Vasquez is interesting. He's _____ teacher.

4. I am bad at French. It's _____ subject.

5. My friend Jaime is tall. He's _____ in the class.

6. He's sporty. I would say he's _____ boy in the school.

WRITING

Find three pictures of different places, people or animals and compare them.

Write a short paragraph. You must use comparatives and superlatives.

Example: *My brother is **funnier than** me, but my sister is **the funniest** in the family.*

Going to

In, on and *at*

Expedition team members trek over blue glacial ice

Going to: Describing future plans

We use *going to* to talk about:

• future plans and arrangements.

Tomorrow we're going to visit a museum.

• something we know is going to happen.

Watch out! That glass is going to fall off the table!

We can use time expressions such as *soon, tomorrow, next week, this evening, in the morning, tonight, at the weekend, later on,* etc. with *going to*.

We're going to paint the sitting room at the weekend.

➔ See grammar box on page 53.

1 **Complete the sentences with *be going to* and the words in brackets.**

Example: *We **are going to visit** my uncle next weekend. (visit)*

1. I _____ my bags tonight. (pack)

2. They _____ lunch on Sunday. (cook)

3. We _____ out late on Saturday evening. (go)

4. We _____ the museum. (not visit)

5. I _____ a present. (bring)

6. I _____ home this evening. (drive)

2 **Match the sentence halves.**

1. We're going to spend   a. how to get to the museum.

2. They're going to find out   b. over the Himalayas.

3. We aren't going to go   c. his class about his trip.

4. They said we're going to fly d. two weeks in Canada.

5. Ellie is going to buy   e. to him about the holiday?

6. Hari is going to tell   f. at the winter games.

7. Are you going to speak   g. to the beach tomorrow.

8. She isn't going to compete   h. souvenirs for everyone.

3 **Put the words in the correct order.**

Example: *are / do / going / at the weekend / to / what / you?*
> ***What are you going to do at the weekend?***

1. I'm / to / going / out / not / go

   _____

2. at / going / I'm / to / homework

   _____

3. are / going / study / what / you / to?

   _____

4. English / going / I'm / for / study / to / test / my

   _____

5. are / going / next week / come / cinema / the / to / to / you?

   _____

6. I'm / yes / that / going / to / do

   _____

7. great / going / be / to / it's

   _____

4 **Add the missing word to each sentence.** Rewrite the sentences.

Example: *I going to visit the mountains with some friends tomorrow.*
> *I **am** going to visit the mountains with some friends tomorrow.*

1. We are going go walking.

   _____

2. We're to leave in the morning.

   _____

3. We are going have lunch on the mountaintop.

   _____

4. We going to come back in the evening.

   _____

5. It's going to be long day.

   _____

6. I'm going to tired when I get back!

   _____

In, on and at: Saying when things happen

In, on and at are prepositions of time.

We use in with months, years, seasons and times of day:

in the morning	in winter
in the afternoon	in June
in the evening	in the holidays
in 1987	

We use on with days and dates:

on Saturdays	on my birthday
on Monday mornings	on Christmas Day
on 5th May	

We usually use at with times, but there are other special uses:

at six o'clock	at the weekend
at midnight	at Christmas
at night	at Easter

1 Write the time expressions in the correct column of the table.

Christmas Day   June   weekdays   2012   the 1960s   5 p.m.

the weekend   half past three   midnight   1st January   Saturdays

the evening   summer   night   last day of every month

in	on	at
	Christmas Day	

2 Complete the sentences with in, on or at.

Example: *He goes to the beach every day **in** the holidays.*

1. _____ the summer, we visit our friends in Spain.

2. He plays football _____ Saturdays.

3. I have a ballet lesson _____ six o'clock.

4. We go on holiday _____ the summer.

5. They often go out _____ the weekend.

6. My birthday is _____ 6th July.

7. She goes away _____ the summer.

8. He wakes up early _____ Sunday mornings.

9. Do you go to bed late _____ night?

10. I always have a cake _____ my birthday.

3 Complete the email with *in*, *on* or *at*.

Subject: Hello from Madrid!

Hi George,

How are you? We're having a good time in Madrid. Yesterday, we went to the Prado museum ____in____ the morning. Then, [1]_____ 11 a.m., we went for a walk in the Retiro Park and watched people rowing boats on the lake. [2]_____ lunchtime, we went over into the centre of town and ate tapas in a small bar. [3]_____ the afternoon, we went to another museum, the Reina Sofia, which had air-conditioning! [4]_____ the evening, it was still hot, but we went for dinner [5]_____ nine o'clock. [6]_____ Tuesday, we are going to Avila, an old walled city outside Madrid.

See you soon,

Albert

---

4 Use the prompts to write sentences about future plans.

Example: *Tuesday / we / go / to the beach*
   On Tuesday, we are going to go to the beach.

1. my sister / play hockey / the weekend

   _____

2. my parents / out for a meal / Friday

   _____

3. my brother / stay in / Saturday night

   _____

4. we / go on holiday / Christmas

   _____

5. we / come back / New Year's Day

   _____

6. school / start / 5th January

   _____

7. it / be difficult getting up / 6.30 a.m. again

   _____

8. but I / enjoy school / winter / because we / play football

   _____

Grammar boxes

Unit 1 *Be*

	Affirmative	Negative	Question	Short answers
I	'm (am)	'm (am) not	Am I?	Yes, I am. No, I'm not.
You / We / They	're (are)	'ren't (are not)	Are ...?	Yes, ... are. No, ... aren't.
He / She / It	's (is)	isn't (is not)	Is ...?	Yes, ... is. No, ... isn't.

Unit 1 *Have got*

	Affirmative	Negative	Question	Short answers
I / You / We / They	've (have) got	haven't (have not) got	Have ... got?	Yes, ... have. No, ... haven't.
He / She / It	's (has) got	hasn't (has not) got	Has ... got?	Yes, ... has. No, ... hasn't.

Unit 2 Present simple

	Affirmative	Negative	Question	Short answers
I / You / We / They	eat	don't (do not) eat	Do ... eat?	Yes, ... do. No, ... don't.
He / She / It	eats	doesn't (does not) eat	Do ... eat?	Yes, ... does. No, ... doesn't.

Unit 5 Present continuous

	Affirmative	Negative	Question	Short answers
I	'm (am) talking	'm not (am not) talking	Am I talking?	Yes, I am. No, I'm not.
He / She / It	's (is) talking	isn't (is not) talking	Is ... talking?	Yes, ... is. No, ... isn't.
You / We / They	're (are) talking	aren't (are not) talking	Are ... talking?	Yes, ... are. No, ... aren't.

Unit 5 *There was* and *there were*

	Affirmative	Negative	Question	Short answers
Past simple	There was There were	There wasn't (was not) There weren't (were not)	Was there ...? Were there ...?	Yes, there was/were. No, there wasn't/weren't.

Unit 6 Past simple

	Affirmative	Negative	Question	Short answers
I / You / He / She / It / We / They	go	didn't (did not) go	Did ... go?	Yes, ... did. No, ... didn't.

Unit 8 *Going to*

	Affirmative	Negative	Question	Short answers
I	'm (am) going to play	'm not (am not) going to play	Am I going to play?	Yes, I am. No, I'm not.
He / She / It	's (is) going to play	isn't (is not) going to play	Is ... going to play?	Yes, ... is. No, ... isn't.
You / We / They	're (are) going to play	aren't (are not) going to play	Are ... going to play?	Yes, ... are. No, ... aren't.

Irregular verbs

Infinitive	Past simple	Past participle	Infinitive	Past simple	Past participle
be	were	been	leave	left	left
beat	beat	beaten	lend	lent	lent
become	became	become	let	let	let
begin	began	begun	lie (down)	lay	lain
bend	bent	bent	light	lit	lit
bet	bet	bet	lose	lost	lost
bite	bit	bitten	make	made	made
bleed	bled	bled	mean	meant	meant
blow	blew	blown	meet	met	met
break	broke	broken	overcome	overcame	overcome
bring	brought	brought	pay	paid	paid
build	built	built	put	put	put
burn	burnt	burnt	quit	quit	quit
buy	bought	bought	read	read	read
carry	carried	carried	ride	rode	ridden
catch	caught	caught	ring	rang	rung
choose	chose	chosen	rise	rose	risen
come	came	come	run	ran	run
cost	cost	cost	say	said	said
cut	cut	cut	see	saw	seen
deal	dealt	dealt	sell	sold	sold
dig	dug	dug	send	sent	sent
dive	dived	dived	set	set	set
do	did	done	sew	sewed	sewn
draw	drew	drawn	shake	shook	shaken
drink	drank	drunk	shine	shone	shone
drive	drove	driven	show	showed	shown
dry	dried	dried	shrink	shrank	shrunk
eat	ate	eaten	shut	shut	shut
fall	fell	fallen	sing	sang	sung
feed	fed	fed	sink	sank	sunk
feel	felt	felt	sit	sat	sat
fight	fought	fought	sleep	slept	slept
find	found	found	slide	slid	slid
flee	fled	fled	speak	spoke	spoken
fly	flew	flown	spend	spent	spent
forbid	forbade	forbidden	spin	spun	spun
forget	forgot	forgotten	stand	stood	stood
forgive	forgave	forgiven	steal	stole	stolen
freeze	froze	frozen	stick	stuck	stuck
fry	fried	fried	sting	stung	stung
get	got	got	stink	stank	stunk
give	gave	given	strike	struck	struck
go	went	gone	swear	swore	sworn
grind	ground	ground	sweep	swept	swept
grow	grew	grown	swim	swam	swum
hang	hung	hung	swing	swung	swung
have	had	had	take	took	taken
hear	heard	heard	teach	taught	taught
hide	hid	hidden	tear	tore	torn
hit	hit	hit	tell	told	told
hold	held	held	think	thought	thought
hurt	hurt	hurt	throw	threw	thrown
keep	kept	kept	understand	understood	understood
kneel	knelt	knelt	wake	woke	woken
knit	knitted	knitted	wear	wore	worn
know	knew	known	weave	wove	woven
lay	laid	laid	win	won	won
lead	led	led	write	wrote	written

NOTES

NOTES